Sisters
as
Friends
Friends
as
Sisters

By Roxie Kelley

With Illustrations by Shelly Reeves Smith

**Andrews McMeel
Publishing**

Kansas City

00 01 02 03 04 TWP 10 9 8 7 6 5 4 3 2 1

ISBN: 0-7407-1067-2

Presented to:

♥

To Jan, for a lifetime of love.
—RGK

To Heather, with love.
—SRS

Contrary to what most of us have been taught, real sisters don't necessarily share the same mother and father... although they might.

It is really a matter, not of common relatives, but of a common heart.

This book
celebrates
sisterhood
in all its forms.
Share it with a
favorite sister...
Share it with
a favorite
friend.

Sisters are linked together through many unseen movements of the heart. Little Moments connect together one ♥ by ♥ one building, growing stronger ♥

A sister
travels with you
always...
She is only
a whisper
or a thought
or
a prayer away...

She
moves through
our
lives
with us...

ou
an
do
this.

Sometimes
we hear
some of her words
slipping
out
of our
own
mouths.

Love
You
♥

I
Miss
You

Let
it
Go!

I
Believe
in
You.

A sister rarely sees
our imperfections,
but
when she does,

she somehow finds them
to be
endearing.

 A sister would never think of trying to change you into becoming someone else...

She would miss the real you too much.

Place Photo Of

The
ReaL
YoU
here.

A sister is gentle with her humor. She laughs with us from deep within, and not just from her mouth.

Laughing
Friends
PHOTO
♥
Here.

A sister never joins your inner critic; she is your most fearless defender against that foe.

Sister never
ever
thinks,
"It must be so
easy for her."

She knows
every difficult path
you have ever
traveled.
She is grateful
for whatever pleasures
come your way.

Love
is
always
the
Solution.

I
Love
you.
♥

Sisters honor
our confusing phases.
They believe
we will make it
to the other side
with a good
measure
of grace.

A sister joins you in your decluttering task. She helps toss out the negative, worrisome thoughts

That bounce around inside your head

Making room for new good thoughts to reside...

She
will even give you
some of her
own

new good thoughts

Good
Thoughts

if you
can't think of any.

When we are
alone
in our darkest
hours,
our sisters come
to sit beside us,
... and light a candle
of hope.

Sisters may
not
always know
what to say
when we are
troubled...

But they know how to be a silent source of strength...

They are not embarrassed by the silence.

They are
a source
of constant
tender
care.

One
of
a
sister's
biggest ♥ wishes
is
for us to find
fulfillment
and joy.

Make a Wish

Sisters lend us courage and their favorite shoes to help us take the next big step.

Place
photo
of
friends
taking
big
steps.

They also
help us
Let Go...
to make
room
for other
possibilities...

To create a space
for
good things
to flow into...

And
that
any little thing
that concerns us
is important enough
for our consideration.

Sisters reserve
time for each other...
not just
leftover time
but real first-rate
first-pick
first-class
time...
and they
look forward to
this time together

... and hold it close to their hearts.

Sisters really believe much of what we have to say is truly fascinating...

They
also believe
that
we have
a
bright and
exciting
future ahead
of us.

Even when
we are
Crabby, Messy,
Fussy, or Lazy

sisters still love us.

And no matter
how young
or
how old
we are,

No matter
if we are finding it
easy   or

difficult

to live with ourselves
at this particular
moment
in time,

No matter what...

We will always need

our sisters.

This we
know
to ♥ be
true.

And
Life is Sweeter

When we have
Sisters as
Friends
and
Friends as
Sisters! ♥

To my
Sister ♥

Photo
of
My Sister,
My Friend...
♥
Here.

Photo
of
My Sister,
My Friend...
♥
Here.